My First Book of Magic Tricks

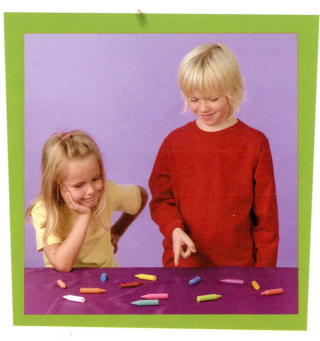

Written by Gordon Hill
Photography by Nigel Goldsmith

p

Contents

Introduction

Doing magic tricks is great fun. There are lots of tricks in this book for you to learn. Try them out in private first.

When you can do a trick really well you can show it to your friends. They will be amazed at your magical skills but do not tell them how the tricks are done. When people know how the tricks are done they will not enjoy them so much.

Have fun with your magic!

Confusing Colours

Two rainbow shapes change their length when you stretch or squeeze them!

You will need:
- two special curved cards

How to make it

1. From a sheet of thin card cut out two rainbow shapes like those shown in the pictures. They must be exactly the same size.

2. Colour one blue and the other red.

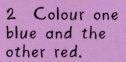

1 Show your audience the red rainbow and then hold the blue one above it. The blue one appears to be shorter than the red one.

2 Pretend to stretch the blue one.

4

3 Show the two rainbows again. This time, however, you hold the red one above the blue one. Now the red one seems to be the shortest.

4 Next pretend to stretch the red one.

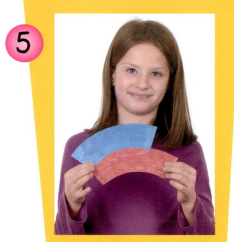

5 Once again hold them both as in step 1. Now the blue one is the shorter of the two!

Now pretend to stretch the blue one and squeeze the red one.

6

7 Hold the two rainbows, one on top of the other, and they are now both the same size!

About Turn

You make an arrow, drawn on a piece of paper, change direction without even touching it!

You will need:
- paper or card
- a pen or pencil
- a jug of water
- a glass tumbler

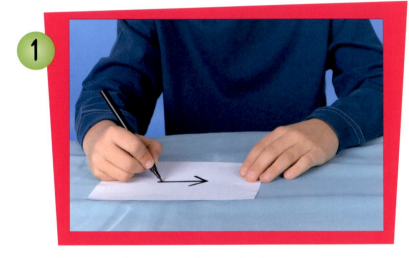

1 Show the card and draw a large arrow on it.

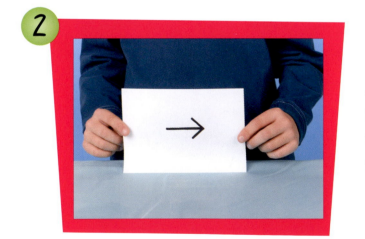

2 Ask your audience if anyone can turn the arrow round without turning the paper around or flipping it over in any way.

When everyone gives up, hold the card behind the glass tumbler – and nothing happens, the arrow is still pointing the same way.

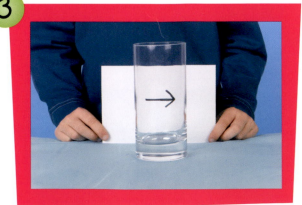

3

4 Now pour some water from the jug into the tumbler.

5 Hold the card to the glass as you did before. Much to everyone's surprise the arrow has now turned around to face the opposite direction!

6 When you take the card away from the tumbler of water the arrow points back to its original direction.

Crafty Knot

Spectators try to tie a knot in a piece of rope without letting go of the ends but this proves to be impossible. You then show how to do it.

1 Show the rope and ask if anyone can tie a knot in it without letting go of the ends.

You will need:
- about a metre of string, rope or ribbon

2 Let several people try but keep a wary eye on them for they may try to tie the knot by letting go of one end quickly in the hope that no one sees this.

3 When everyone has given up all you do is lay the rope out on the table.

4 Now cross your arms.

5 Keeping your arms crossed, pick up one end of the rope with your left hand.

6 Pick up the other end of the rope with your right hand.

7 Keep hold of the ends of the rope as you unfold your arms and the knot will form itself in the centre of the rope!

Colour Sense

Someone chooses a crayon while your back is turned. Without seeing any of the crayons you announce what colour has been chosen.

You will need:
• a box of coloured wax crayons

Tip the crayons onto a table.

Ask someone to pick up any crayon while your back is turned and to remove all the other crayons out of sight.

Now ask the spectator to hand you the crayon behind your back.

Turn to face the audience, keeping the crayon behind your back. Dig your thumbnail into the crayon to scrape off a small amount.

Bring your right hand forward and up to your forehead as if concentrating deeply.

As you do this, quickly glance at your thumbnail and you will know what colour has been chosen. Announce the chosen colour as dramatically as you can and then bring the crayon into view to show that you are right.

Tip: As a general rule you should never repeat a trick but this one is worth doing more than once to prove that it wasn't a fluke – but remember to secretly wipe the first colour from your nail before you do it again.

It's Magic

Show how a pencil can pass through a handkerchief without harming the material.

You will need:
* a pencil
* a handkerchief

1

Spread the handkerchief out on the table with one of the corners pointing towards you (this is marked A in the picture).

2

Put the pencil on the handkerchief.

3

Pick up the corner nearest to you (A) and fold it away from you over the pencil and slightly beyond the furthest corner (B).

12

4 Roll the middle of the handkerchief around the pencil. Keep rolling until the far corner comes into view. As soon as this happens stop rolling.

B

A

Take corners A and B and pull them in opposite directions until the handkerchief is out flat again.

5

B

A

6 The pencil seems to have disappeared but then you lift up the handkerchief to show that it has gone right through the material!

Making Money

You put three coins in your hand. When you open your hand there are six coins!

Secret preparation

Hide three coins under the cover of the magazine.

Lay the magazine on a table with three coins hidden inside. Show the three other coins.

1

2

Place them, one at a time, on the cover of the magazine.

3  Pick up the magazine with your right hand.

Bend the magazine a little and tip the three coins from the cover into your left hand.

4

5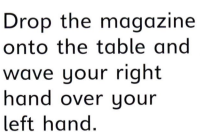

The audience do not see the three hidden coins which slip out from the magazine and into your hand at the same time.

6

Drop the magazine onto the table and wave your right hand over your left hand.

7 Slowly open your left hand and allow the coins to drop, one at a time, onto the table. The three coins have multiplied to six!

Ribbon from Nowhere

You show both your hands are empty then produce a long coloured ribbon from nowhere!

You will need:
• a long ribbon
• a small piece of sticky tape

Secret preparation

Before showing this trick you must wind the ribbon, as neatly as you can, around your right thumb. When you reach the end of the ribbon use a small piece of sticky tape to stop it from unrolling.

1 Keep your thumb, with the ribbon on it, hidden until you want to show this trick. If you have pockets in your clothes the easiest thing to do is to keep your hand in a pocket until you are ready.

2 Face your audience and hold up your left hand.

Take your right hand from your pocket and, keeping your thumb bent inwards so the ribbon cannot be seen, bring it up behind your left hand. Then open up your right thumb behind the left hand. To the audience it seems that your hands are empty.

3

Bring both hands together, palm to palm, with both thumbs tucked inside.

5 Using the left thumb and first finger, pull off the tape.

4

6 Now pull the ribbon out from your hands and your audience will have no idea where it came from.

17

Painless Operation

Remove part of your left thumb and then put it back again!

1

Hold the left hand so the back of the hand is facing the audience.

2

Bring your right hand above the left until the fingers cover the left thumb.

Under cover of the right fingers bend both thumbs inwards and place the right thumb against the left.

3

The join between the two bent thumbs is hidden behind the right forefinger so that from the front it looks like one ordinary thumb.

4

5 Move your hand to the right, keeping the thumb against the top of the left forefinger. It looks as if you have broken off half of your thumb.

6

Pause for just a second and then move the right hand back to the left thumb.

Open both hands at the same time and your left thumb is seen to be fully restored.

7

Molecular Magic

A wooden pencil is turned to rubber and then sticks to your hand by magic.

1 Hold the pencil at one end between the finger and thumb of your right hand.

2 Hold it loosely as you shake your hand up and down, at the same time allowing the pencil to rock between your fingers.

3 The pencil looks very floppy, as if it is made of rubber. Tell your audience that this shaking causes the molecular structure of the pencil to change.

Hold the pencil in your left hand and grasp your left wrist with the right hand. The back of your left hand must be facing the audience.

4

5

Secretly straighten your right forefinger so it holds the pencil against the palm of your left hand.

You can now open the fingers of your left hand and the pencil appears to be sticking to it by some strange magnetic force. Tell your audience that heating the pencil by shaking it has made it rather sticky so it clings to your hand.

6

Incredible Escape

A coin escapes from beneath a tumbler without being touched.

1 Place the two large coins on the table, a short distance apart from one another.

2 Put the small coin between the other two.

3 Now place the tumbler upside down, so it is balanced on the two outer coins.

4 Tell your audience that the small coin is now imprisoned and that there is no way of getting it out from beneath the tumbler without lifting the tumbler.

5 Cover the glass with the handkerchief but place it so it is not touching the tablecloth at the rear of the tumbler.

6 Keep talking and waving your left hand over the covered tumbler. As you do so, secretly scratch the tablecloth a short distance behind the tumbler.

7 This scratching will cause the small coin to move out from beneath the tumbler. When it is completely clear of the tumbler you can lift off the handkerchief to show that the coin has escaped.

Linking Clips

Two paper clips are put on a slip of paper. They are nowhere near each other but when the paper is pulled taut they leap off and link together in mid-air.

You will need:
• two paper clips
• a piece of paper (14 cm x 8 cm)

1

Fold over about one third of the left end of the paper, as shown.

2

Place one of the clips over the two thicknesses of paper created by the fold.

3

Now fold over the right end of the paper, as shown.

4 Put the second clip over the two layers of paper nearest the audience.

5 Hold up the paper and point out that the clips are nowhere near each other.

6 Pull your hands outwards sharply - the right hand to the right and the left hand to the left.

7 The paper clips will leap off the paper and link themselves together!

Through the Looking Glass

You show a picture of a mirror and then, by cutting the picture in a special way, go through it!

How to make it
Draw a picture of a large mirror on a piece of A4 paper.

You will need:
• A4 paper
• a pencil or pen
• scissors

1 Show the picture of the mirror and say that you are going to walk through it.

2 Fold the paper in half, lengthways.

Use the scissors to make several cuts in the folded paper, as shown.

Next make some more cuts from the opposite edges of the folded paper, as shown. These cuts go between the first cuts you made.

Now open out the paper and cut along the central fold, as shown.

Carefully open out the paper and it will make a big loop that will go easily over your head.

Step into the loop and pull it upwards over your body!

With special thanks to our models Phoebe Brook, Sonny Murphy, Rebecca Morgan, Daniel Richards, Tyler Gane and Loui Gane.

This is a Parragon book
This edition published 2006

Parragon
Queen Street House
4 Queen Street
Bath BA1 1HE, UK

Copyright © Parragon Books Ltd 2006

ISBN 1-40544-741-9
Printed in China